Cooking for Gold

Produced by Marjorie Poore Productions

Photographs by Alec Fatalevich

RECIPES FROM THE PUBLIC TELEVISION SHOW

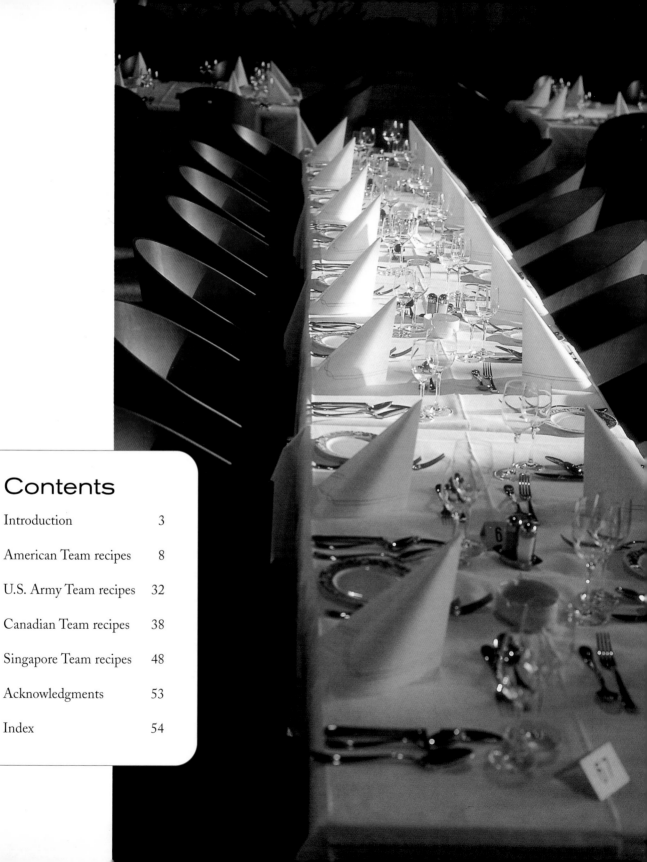

Contents

Introduction

Every four years for the last century, without much fanfare or media attention, the world's greatest chefs have gathered in Germany for what insiders call the "culinary olympics." Chefs regard it as the most prestigious and grueling cooking competition in the world, attracting teams from every part of the globe. Just like their sports counterparts, the competing teams train for years—designing and perfecting their recipes and planning their every move in the kitchen for the actual competition. The last event took place in 2000 in Erfurt, Germany.

More than 900 chefs competed, bringing a variety of cuisines and skill levels to the event. Chefs could enter four different competitions: national, military, youth, and regional. The competition with the highest profile pitted the national teams, representing twenty-eight countries with one team per country, against each other. The team members were carefully chosen, usually by their country's professional chef organization. The military competition drew fourteen international teams, including the United States Army Culinary Arts Team. The youth competition challenged chefs under the age of 21 and the regional team competitions were open to just about any chef group that wanted to test their skills in this international forum.

Each team had to compete in four areas of cooking: Hot Food, Appetizers, Menu of the Day, and Pastry. Probably the most intense contest was the Hot Food Competition, which required each team to prepare 110 three-course meals in a five-hour window. While most of the meals were served to paying customers, the judges randomly picked a plate from the assembly line for scoring. Besides being judged on their dishes' taste,

U.S. ARMY

AMERICA

CANADA

SINGAPORE

SWEDEN

SWITZERLAND

VERBAND DER KÖCHE DEUTSCHLANDS e.V.

Köche-Nationalmannschaft

German National Culinary Team VKD

OFFICIAL SPONSOR

4. SALON CULINAIRE MONDIAL 1999
BASEL / SWITZERLAND

HUNGARY

GERMANY

the teams were judged on cooking techniques, cleanliness, their *mise en place* (setup), and organization. Judges were even seen inspecting garbage cans to find out if the teams had wasted too many ingredients, a veritable sin in the world of cooking.

In the remaining three categories, Appetizers, Menu of the Day, and Pastry, the foods were presented as *garde manger*, or cold food buffets, and displayed on elegantly designed tables, bursting with artistry and creativity. Among chefs, these displays are a time-honored tradition dating back

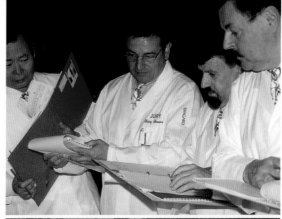

to the Renaissance. They paint the food with a layer of aspic gelée, which not only makes the food glisten, but also preserves and protects it. Because of the exorbitant costs in preparing these *garde manger* foods, they're rarely found in restaurants anymore, but the tradition is kept alive in competitions such as this.

The U.S. national team entered under the auspices of the American Culinary Federation, the largest professional chef organization in America. All the U.S. teams, including the military team, have always performed very well in the "culinary olympics" and are regarded as some of the strongest teams on the circuit. While the public has become very familiar with the media chefs who have dominated the airwaves and bookstores over the last twenty years, competition chefs are a less familiar breed. These highly skilled and exceedingly talented chefs participate strictly out of love for their profession and pride in representing their country, and for the tremendous experience this kind of competition gives them. They volunteer for this competition and are sometimes not even compensated for the time they must take from their paid work for practice sessions. Nor are there any lucrative sponsorship contracts waiting for them at the end of the competition. But they do go home with (hopefully) a few gold medals and new skills that take them to a higher level of cooking. Just walking the halls of this culinary contest, with its extraordinary displays of international foods, is an incomparable experience for chefs of this caliber.

This book contains recipes from several of the U.S. teams we followed (the national and the military teams). We were also very fortunate to get recipes from the Canadian team, another top gold medal winner on the circuit with a strong reputation. In each case, we asked them to give us recipes tailored for a home cook or simplified versions of the competition recipes. We hope you enjoy them.

—Marjorie Poore, *Producer*

Parmesan Dijon Crostini Gratinée

1 cup plus 2 tablespoons grated best-quality Parmesan cheese

2 tablespoons Dijon mustard

2 tablespoons fresh chopped chives

½ cup best-quality mayonnaise

Freshly ground black pepper to taste

8 slices French bread, diagonally cut about ¼ inch thick and toasted

1 tablespoon finely chopped fresh parsley

★ Preheat broiler and line a baking sheet with foil. In a small bowl of an electric mixer fitted with the whisk attachment, whisk together 1 cup of the cheese, mustard, chives, and mayonnaise at low speed until well combined. Season with pepper. (Cheese mixture may be made up to 2 days ahead and chilled, covered.)

★ Spread cheese mixture evenly over bread slices and sprinkle with the remaining Parmesan. Arrange crostini on a baking sheet or the rack of a broiler pan. Set the pan about 3 inches from the heat and broil crostini until golden brown and cheese is heated through, about 1 to 2 minutes. Transfer crostini to a serving platter and sprinkle with parsley. *Makes 8 crostini*

Glazed Golden Beets

1 pound golden beets
(tennis ball size)

2 tablespoons granulated sugar

Dash whole cloves

Dash allspice

1 bay leaf

¼ cinnamon stick

2½ teaspoons aged sherry vinegar

½ cup water

RED PICKLED ONIONS

⅛ cup plus ½ teaspoon water

⅛ cup plus ½ teaspoon apple syrup

⅛ teaspoon chopped dill stems,
tied in a cheesecloth sachet

¾ cup finely julienned red onions

★ Preheat the oven to 375°F (190°C). Wash beets and dry roast ¾ of them on baking sheets for 50 minutes to 1 hour until completely cooked.

★ Dice the remaining beets and place in a heavy stockpot with the remaining ingredients. Simmer for 1 hour, or until a rich syrupy consistency is reached. Strain and reserve the glaze.

★ To make the pickled onions, combine the water, apple syrup, sachet, and onions in a saucepan and simmer until al dente and the liquid has reduced by half.

★ Peel roasted beets and slice each into 6 wedges. Top with the strained glaze and pickled onions and serve. *Serves 8*

¼ cup chopped apple-smoked bacon

1 cup peeled and diced celery stalks

1 cup split and finely diced baby leeks (stalk and center only)

½ cup chardonnay

2 cups sweet white corn, shaved from the cob and simmered in chicken broth until tender

2 cups heavy cream that has been simmered with chopped corncobs, reduced to 1 cup, then strained

Salt and freshly ground white pepper to taste

2 tablespoons clarified butter

1 tablespoon white truffle oil

6 Nantucket Diver scallops (or day boat sea scallops, dry packed), muscles removed

1 tablespoon coriander dust (coriander seed lightly toasted and ground with salt and pepper)

LOBSTER FRITTERS

2 eggs

1 tablespoon salad oil

1 cup milk

4 teaspoons baking powder

1 teaspoon salt

⅛ teaspoon Old Bay Seasoning

2 cups flour

1 cup cooked and chopped lobster meat

2 tablespoons chopped flat-leaf parsley

½ cup grated white Cheddar cheese

Soybean or canola oil for frying

2 tablespoons snipped fresh chives, for garnish

Coriander-Crusted Nantucket Diver Scallops
WITH CORN CREAM AND BABY LEEK STEW AND LOBSTER FRITTERS

★ In a large skillet over medium-high heat, sweat the bacon until slightly crisp. Add the celery and leeks and stir for 2 to 3 minutes. Add chardonnay and cook to reduce slightly. Stir in the corn and corn cream, and simmer for 3 to 5 minutes. Season with salt and white pepper.

★ Heat a sauté pan over high heat and add the clarified butter and truffle oil. Rub the scallops with coriander dust and season with salt and pepper. Sear scallops in the butter and truffle oil until well caramelized on both sides.

★ To make lobster fritters, in a large bowl, combine the eggs, oil, milk, baking powder, salt, seasoning, and flour. Mix well to remove lumps. Fold in lobster, parsley, and grated cheese.

★ Heat about ½ inch of oil in a skillet over high heat. Drop the batter by the teaspoonful into the hot oil and fry the fritters for 2 to 3 minutes, until golden brown and crispy. Remove and drain on paper towels for 1 to 2 minutes.

★ Spoon the corn and leek stew into soup plates. Place a scallop in the center and garnish each bowl with 3 fritters. Sprinkle with snipped chives and serve immediately. *Serves 6*

Charred Corn and Sweet Potato Chowder
WITH SHRIMP

5 ears white corn, shucked and cleaned

1 medium green bell pepper

2 large red bell peppers

1 small leek

1 medium red onion

1½ pounds sweet potatoes, cut into 2-inch chunks

½ cup best-quality olive oil

4 cloves garlic, peeled and minced

1 stalk celery, finely diced

3 quarts shrimp stock

1 tablespoon chopped fresh basil

1 bay leaf

1 teaspoon chopped fresh thyme

1 pound small shrimp, peeled and deveined (reserve shells for another use)

1 quart heavy cream

Salt and freshly ground white pepper to taste

★ Prepare and heat a charcoal grill to medium high. Place corn, bell peppers, leek, and onion on the grill and cook until the vegetables are charred golden brown. Remove vegetables from the grill and place the bell peppers in a paper bag to steam. When cool, remove the skins, all seeds, and stems from the peppers and finely dice. When the corn is slightly cooled, cut off the kernels from the cobs and set the corn aside. In a large saucepan, boil the sweet potatoes until fork tender. Drain and cool. Peel the sweet potatoes, finely dice, and set aside. Dice the charred onion and leek the same size as the sweet potatoes and set aside.

★ Heat the olive oil in a stockpot and sauté the garlic and celery over moderate heat until the celery is translucent in color. Add the shrimp stock and fresh basil, bay leaf, and thyme. Increase heat to medium high and bring to a simmer. Add corn, sweet potatoes, bell peppers, leeks, and onions. Cook for 25 minutes.

★ Add the peeled and cleaned shrimp and stir to cook the shrimp. Reduce heat and add the heavy cream. At any stage of the cooking process, do not boil the chowder. Season with salt and pepper and serve hot. *Serves 8*

Meat from 4 (1½-pound) lobsters, poached

¼ cup vanilla oil

3 basil leaves, cut into chiffonade

1 fennel bulb, shaved

20 sections red grapefruit

2 small red onions, very thinly sliced

20 grape tomatoes

4 ounces baby penne pasta

CURRY VANILLA VINAIGRETTE

10 tablespoons (5 ounces) virgin olive oil

¼ cup chopped shallot

¼ cup finely diced carrot

¼ cup finely diced celery root

⅜ cup (3 ounces) dry white wine

1½ tablespoons Madras curry powder

½ vanilla bean, split

1 tablespoon minced fresh sage

½ cup chicken broth

¼ cup lobster broth

⅜ cup (3 ounces) champagne vinegar

Salt and pepper to taste

2 tablespoons diced papaya

Composed Insalata of Lobster and Penne Pasta
IN A CURRY VANILLA VINAIGRETTE

★ To make the salad, toss the lobster meat with oil and basil. Mix fennel, grapefruit, onions, and tomatoes. Cook pasta until firm but tender; drain. (Do not rinse.)

★ To make the vinaigrette, heat 2 tablespoons of the oil and cook the shallot, carrot, and celery root until soft. Add the wine, curry powder, vanilla bean, and sage and cook until reduced. Add both broths and simmer until reduced by a half. Strain and let cool. With an electric whisk, whisk in the remaining olive oil and vinegar until it emulsifies. Season with salt and pepper and adjust consistency with warm water, if necessary. Add papaya.

★ Toss the pasta with the fruit and vegetable mixture and 6 ounces of the vinaigrette. Place on a plate and dress with the lobster and remaining vinaigrette. *Serves 4*

CABERNET-ORANGE BUTTER

½ cup unsalted butter

1 (750-milliliter) bottle Beaulieu Vineyard cabernet sauvignon or other cabernet sauvignon

1 tablespoon sugar

2 tablespoons fresh tarragon

1 tablespoon orange zest

1 teaspoon kosher salt

1 teaspoon black pepper

1 pound Yukon Gold potatoes

1 tablespoon salt

3 quarts water

1 cup butter, melted

2 teaspoons salt

1 teaspoon black pepper

2 teaspoons truffle oil (optional)

2 tablespoons grated Parmigiano-Reggiano cheese

Savory Potato Waffle
WITH BEAULIEU VINEYARD CABERNET-ORANGE BUTTER

★ To make the Cabernet-Orange Butter, place butter in a medium-sized stainless steel bowl and allow to soften at room temperature for approximately 2 hours.

★ In a medium-sized stainless steel saucepan over medium-low heat, add the cabernet and sugar and gently reduce wine by 90%, being sure not to scorch the wine. The wine will become syrupy. Allow the syrup to cool slightly before adding it to the softened butter. Add the remaining ingredients and mix well.

★ To make the waffle, wash and peel the potatoes. Boil them in salted water until they are cooked but still firm. Use a toothpick to test. Drain potatoes and let them air-dry until completely cool. With a large-slotted grater, grate the potatoes.

★ Add ½ cup melted butter, salt, pepper, truffle oil (if using), and cheese to the potatoes and gently mix. Do not overmix the potato mixture.

★ Preheat a waffle iron and brush with melted butter. Place the potato mixture on the waffle iron, spreading the mixture evenly over the bottom surface of the iron. Close the lid and gently press shut. Cook until the waffle is golden brown, approximately 15 minutes. Do not check the waffle too soon, but allow to cook for at least 10 minutes before raising the lid.

★ Cut the waffle into 4 pieces and serve hot with Cabernet-Orange Butter. *Serves 4*

3 tablespoons olive oil

3 tablespoons apricot preserves

1½ tablespoons white wine vinegar

2½ teaspoons Dijon mustard

2¼ teaspoons curry powder

1¼ teaspoons minced garlic

Salt to taste

24 jumbo dry-pack scallops

1 bunch cilantro, for garnish

lemon zest, for garnish

Skewered Jumbo Scallops
WITH APRICOT CURRY GLAZE

★ Whisk together the oil, apricot preserves, vinegar, mustard, curry powder, garlic, and salt in a large bowl. Add scallops and toss well to coat. Cover and refrigerate for at least 1 hour.

★ Meanwhile, soak six to eight 10-inch bamboo skewers in water to cover for 30 minutes. Prepare a charcoal grill to medium-high heat. Thread 3 or 4 scallops per skewer and grill just until cooked through and scallops are firm, about 3 minutes per side. Remove skewers from grill and place on a serving platter. Garnish with cilantro and lemon zest. *Serves 6 to 8*

1 cup panko bread crumbs

½ cup grated horseradish

½ teaspoon chopped fresh thyme

1 teaspoon snipped chives

1 teaspoon snipped fresh rosemary

1 teaspoon chopped parsley

½ cup seasoned flour

1 egg, whipped with 1 tablespoon milk

6 (6- to 8-ounce) halibut fillets

Whipped Yukon Gold potatoes

Diced tomato, for garnish

Chive oil, for garnish

Halibut
IN HORSERADISH CRUST

★ In a shallow bowl, combine bread crumbs, horseradish, fresh herbs, and mix well.

★ Place the seasoned flour in another shallow bowl or on a plate. Dip the fish fillets into the egg mixture and then into the seasoned flour. Dip again into the egg mixture and finally into the bread crumb mix.

★ Preheat the oven to 350°F (177°C).

★ In a large ovenproof skillet over medium-high heat, pan sear the fish lightly, until well caramelized. Place the skillet in the oven and bake for 6 to 8 minutes. Serve the halibut with whipped Yukon Gold potatoes and garnish with diced tomato and chive oil. *Serves 6*

Chicken Breast in Lentil and Vegetable Ragout
WITH BRAISED MUSTARD GREENS AND CANDIED CHESTNUTS

4 (6- to 8-ounce) skinless chicken breasts with wing, frenched (breast meat removed from bone to first joint of the wing)

¼ cup canola oil

1 tablespoon Southwestern seasoning

½ cup pearl onions, pared

½ cup peeled and diced carrots

½ cup peeled and diced celery

½ cup peeled and diced Jerusalem artichokes

½ cup peeled and diced celery root

¼ cup olive oil

Salt and pepper to taste

½ cup cabernet sauvignon

1 teaspoon thyme leaves

1 cup lentils, parcooked in chicken stock

1 cup veal stock

1 teaspoon fresh tarragon leaves, destemmed and thinly sliced crosswise

¼ cup crème fraîche

½ cup finely diced slab bacon

½ cup finely diced Spanish onion

2 cups mustard greens, cleaned and blanched in salted water

1 cup chicken stock

¼ cup chestnuts, roasted, shelled, and lightly candied in apple cider and honey

1 tablespoon snipped chives, for garnish

★ Rub chicken breasts with ½ of the canola oil and the Southwestern seasoning. Marinate, covered, for 30 to 45 minutes in the refrigerator.

★ Preheat the oven to 400°F (205°C). Toss pearl onions and diced root vegetables in olive oil, salt, and pepper. Place on a baking sheet and roast for 15 to 20 minutes, or until lightly caramelized but still al dente. Cool and reserve.

★ Warm a sauté pan over medium-high heat and place remaining canola oil in pan. Add chicken breasts and sear lightly on both sides. Remove from pan and place on a dish. Add caramelized root vegetables, cabernet, and thyme to the pan, and cook to reduce wine by a half.

★ Add lentils, veal stock, and chicken to the pan. For 15 to 20 minutes, simmer on top of the stove or place, uncovered, in a preheated 325°F (163°C) oven. Adjust seasoning and add tarragon and crème fraîche. Reserve.

★ In a sauté pan over medium heat, sweat the bacon until lightly golden. Add diced Spanish onion and sauté until translucent. Add mustard greens and chicken stock, and simmer until greens are tender. Add candied chestnuts and season with salt and pepper.

★ To serve, spoon 4 ounces of Lentil and Vegetable Ragout onto the center of the plate; top with braised greens. Slice each chicken breast and arrange around the greens. Garnish with snipped chives.
Serves 4

Beaulieu Vineyard Crispy Game Hen

8 game hens

1 tablespoon plus ¾ cup kosher salt

3 tablespoons tinted cure mix
(see note)

½ gallon cold water

1 tablespoon pickling spice

2 cups honey

1 cinnamon stick

½ cup brown sugar

3 cups balsamic vinegar

1 cup low-sodium soy sauce

1 cup molasses

4 sprigs fresh thyme

★ Clean, wash, and towel dry game hens. Sprinkle with 1 table-spoon kosher salt, truss with 2 feet of butcher's twine, and reserve in the refrigerator.

★ In a stainless steel saucepan, combine the tinted cure mix, cold water, pickling spice, 1 cup honey, ¾ cup kosher salt, cinnamon stick, and brown sugar and bring to a boil. Skim off any impurities that rise to the surface and discard. Allow this brine to cool completely before using.

★ Once the brine has cooled, place the hens into the brine and refrigerate for 3 hours.

★ Combine the vinegar, soy sauce, molasses, 1 cup honey, and thyme sprigs and bring to a rolling boil. While the solution is boiling, remove the hens from the brine and dip each hen into the boiling solution 4 times. Drain the hens well and hang in the refrigerator for 24 hours.

★ Once the hens have air-dried, preheat the oven to 375°F (190°C). Place hens on a roasting rack fitted with a drip pan, and roast until the hens are golden brown, remembering to baste the hens with the pan drippings every 15 minutes. Remove from the oven and serve. *Serves 4*

NOTE: Tinted cure mix can be purchased from The Sausage Maker, Inc., 1500 Clinton Street, Building 123, Buffalo, NY 14206, 1-888-490-8525.

Braised Veal Rack

2 (1-pound) baby veal racks

1 teaspoon caraway seeds

1 teaspoon coriander

1 teaspoon thyme

1 teaspoon sage

Kosher salt

2 tablespoons olive oil

½ cup finely minced shallots

¼ cup finely minced carrots

¼ cup finely minced celery root

3 cloves garlic, finely minced

2 tablespoons tomato paste

1 cup red wine

2 plum tomatoes, peeled, seeded, and diced

2 cups brown veal stock

1 bay leaf

Sections of 1 lemon

Juice of 1 lemon

Sections of 1 blood orange

Juice of 1 blood orange

2 tablespoons butter

Freshly ground black pepper

2 tablespoons chopped parsley, for garnish

★ Preheat the oven to 275°F (133°C).

★ French-cut the racks by removing meat from the bones and trimming well for presentation. Tie the racks with butcher's twine to help hold the shape while braising.

★ Place the caraway seeds, coriander, thyme, and sage in a coffee or spice grinder and grind well to make a spice rub. Season the veal with kosher salt and this dry rub.

★ In a heavy-bottomed shallow pot, over medium heat, heat the olive oil and sear the racks on both sides until well caramelized. Remove racks from the pot to a plate. Add the shallots, carrots, celery root, and garlic to the pot and sauté until lightly caramelized. Stir in the tomato paste and cook the vegetables until lightly browned. (The natural sugars in the vegetables will brown nicely in the tomato paste.) Deglaze the pan with the red wine, scraping the browned bits from the bottom of the pot. After cooking for 2 or 3 minutes, add the diced plum tomatoes. Add the veal stock and bay leaf and simmer for 2 or 3 more minutes.

★ Place the veal racks back into the pot and braise in the oven for 1 to 1½ hours, until the veal is very tender. Remove the racks from the braising pan to a serving platter and cover with foil to keep warm. Place the pan back on the stove over medium heat and add the sections and juice of lemon, the sections and juice of blood orange, and the butter and heat thoroughly. Season to taste with salt and pepper. Remove the twine from the veal. Spoon the sauce over the veal, sprinkle with chopped parsley, and serve immediately. *Serves 4*

VANILLA CINNAMON ICE CREAM

1 vanilla bean

2 ¼ cups milk

4 ½ ounces egg yolks (about 9 yolks)

Pinch of salt

1 cup (7 ounces) sugar

¾ cup cream

2 ½ teaspoons cinnamon

GANACHE SAUCE

1 ¾ cup cream

14 ounces semisweet chocolate

2 tablespoons coffee liqueur

CHOCOLATE MOUSSE CAKE

1 pound semisweet chocolate

1 cup heavy cream

6 eggs

1 teaspoon vanilla extract

5 tablespoons (2 ½ ounces) sugar

3 tablespoons (1 ½ ounces) cake flour

3 tablespoons coffee liqueur

Warm Chocolate Mousse Cake WITH VANILLA CINNAMON ICE CREAM AND GANACHE SAUCE

★ To make the ice cream, scrape the vanilla seeds from the bean into the milk in a saucepan and scald the milk. Mix the yolks, salt, and sugar together in another saucepan. Slowly pour the hot milk into the egg mixture while stirring. Continue to cook until the custard coats the back of a spoon. Add the cream and cinnamon. Process in an ice cream maker according to the manufacturer's directions. Keep frozen until needed.

★ To make the sauce, in a saucepan, scald the cream. Chop chocolate into small pieces and place in a separate saucepan over low heat. Pour hot cream over the chocolate and stir until all the chocolate has melted. Add liqueur. Keep warm.

★ To make the cake, preheat the oven to 325°F (163°C). Grease 12 large timbales or custard cups. Melt chocolate and ½ cup cream together in the top of a double boiler and set aside.

★ Mix eggs, vanilla, sugar, and flour together at high speed for 10 minutes. Temper chocolate mixture by folding in ⅓ of the egg mixture. Then fold the rest of egg mixture in.

★ Whip the remaining ½ cup cream to soft peaks and fold into the chocolate and egg mixture. Add coffee liqueur. Pour batter into the greased timbales and bake for 8 to 10 minutes, or until the cake feels firm to the touch. Let cool for 3 minutes.

★ To serve, unmold a warm mousse cake and place on a plate with a scoop of ice cream. Drizzle warm sauce on top of the cake and ice cream. *Serves 12*

ALMOND CAKE

16 ounces almond paste

1½ cups sugar

1 cup unsalted butter

6 eggs

1 teaspoon orange extract

Grated zest of 1 orange

1 tablespoon (½ ounce) flour

½ cup dried cranberries

¼ cup shelled pistachios

CITRUS SYRUP

1 cup sugar

¾ cup water

Juice of 1 orange

Juice of 1 lemon

¼ cup citrus liqueur (Triple Sec, Cointreau, etc.)

Whipped cream

Orange marmalade

Cranberry, Orange, and Pistachio Almond Cake
WITH CITRUS SYRUP

★ To make the cake, preheat the oven to 375°F (190°C) and grease a 9-inch round cake pan.

★ In an electric mixer with the paddle attachment, cream together the almond paste, sugar, and butter. Add the eggs one at a time, making sure to incorporate each egg fully before adding another. Add the orange extract and zest and mix. Then incorporate the flour and mix until smooth. Fold in the cranberries and pistachios and place the batter in the prepared cake pan.

★ Bake for 35 to 40 minutes, or until a toothpick inserted in the middle of the cake comes out clean. Let the cake cool on a rack in the pan for 10 minutes, and then flip the cake out of the pan onto a serving plate.

★ To make the syrup, combine all the ingredients except the liqueur. Bring the mixture to a simmer, and then remove from the heat. Let the mixture cool slightly. While the syrup and the cake are still warm, add the liqueur and soak the almond cake.

★ Serve the almond cake with whipped cream and a spoonful of orange marmalade. *Makes one 9-inch cake*

Banana Turnovers

TURNOVER DOUGH

½ cup butter

½ cup cream cheese

¾ cup granulated sugar

1 teaspoon vanilla extract

1 egg yolk

1 cup plus 2 tablespoons bread flour

¼ teaspoon salt

1 egg beaten with 2 tablespoons water to make an egg wash

1 cup confectioners' sugar

BANANA FILLING

2 bananas

2 tablespoons butter

¼ cup brown sugar

Juice of 1 lemon

Juice of 2 oranges

2 tablespoons dark rum

1 teaspoon cinnamon

1 vanilla bean

★ To make the dough, cream together the butter, cream cheese, and ½ cup granulated sugar. Add the vanilla extract and the egg yolk and mix well. Add the bread flour and salt and mix slightly. Turn out onto a floured work surface and knead to bring the dough together. Wrap the dough in plastic wrap and refrigerate for 3 hours.

★ To make the filling, peel and cut the bananas into ½-inch dice. In a sauté pan over medium heat, melt the butter and the brown sugar together. Deglaze the pan with the lemon and orange juices and the rum. Add the bananas, cinnamon, and the seeds of the vanilla bean and stir to coat the bananas. (The vanilla pod can be saved for another use or used to make vanilla sugar.) Cook the bananas until they are warmed through but still slightly firm. Place the filling in the refrigerator to chill.

★ To assemble the turnovers, roll the turnover dough to ¼-inch thickness and cut 3- to 4-inch disks with a round cookie cutter. Brush the edges of the disks with the egg wash. Place a small amount of banana filling in the center of each disk and fold the dough in half, encasing the filling in a half-circle shape. Pinch the edges together to seal. Place the turnovers on a parchment-lined baking sheet and refrigerate for 15 minutes.

★ Preheat the oven to 350°F (177°C). Brush the turnovers lightly with egg wash and sprinkle with the remaining ¼ cup granulated sugar. Bake for 10 to 15 minutes until golden brown. Allow to cool slightly and dust with confectioners' sugar. Serve warm. *Makes 20 turnovers*

ROASTED PEARS

2 Bosc pears

1 vanilla bean

1 cup sweet dessert wine

1 cinnamon stick (optional)

¼ cup sugar

¼ cup butter, cut into small pieces

CREME BRULEE

2 cups heavy cream

¼ cup milk

½ cup sugar

1 vanilla bean

6 egg yolks

Roasted Pear Crème Brûlée

★ To prepare the pears, preheat the oven to 350°F (177°C). Peel and cut the pears in half. Remove the core with a melon baller and place the pear halves in a baking dish with the flat side of the pears down.

★ Split the vanilla bean and scrape the seeds into the wine. Stir until the beans break up. Pour the wine mixture over the pears and place the vanilla pod and the cinnamon stick in the baking dish.

★ Sprinkle the pears with the sugar and pieces of butter. Roast them, covered, until a paring knife can pierce a pear easily and the pear is soft. (Cooking time will depend on the ripeness of the pears.) Baste the pears with the cooking liquid often during baking. Remove the pears and allow them to cool. When they are cool, dice them.

★ To make the crème brûlée, preheat the oven to 300°F (149°C). Divide the diced pears into four 6-ounce crème brûlée dishes. Place the dishes in an ovenproof pan and fill the pan with water to halfway up the sides of the dishes.

★ Combine the cream, milk, and sugar in a saucepan. Slice the vanilla bean, scrape the seeds, and add the seeds and vanilla pod to the cream mixture. Over medium-high heat, scald the cream mixture and remove the pan from the heat. Pour out ½ cup of the cream mixture into a shallow bowl and whisk in the egg yolks. Pour this back into the cream mixture and stir to blend well. Strain the custard through a fine-mesh sieve. Divide this mixture equally among the four dishes of pears and cover the dishes with aluminum foil.

★ Bake the custards for 30 to 45 minutes until set. Let cool and chill overnight, covered, in the refrigerator.

★ When ready to serve, sprinkle the tops of the crème brûlée with sugar and caramelize under a broiler or kitchen torch until the tops are browned and crispy. *Serves 4*

U.S. Army Team

Yellow Pepper and Cheese Terrine

2 teaspoons unflavored gelatin

¼ cup vegetable broth or chicken stock

1 large yellow bell pepper, roasted, skinned, and cut to fit terrine pan

6 ounces cream cheese

1 tablespoon finely chopped parsley

1 teaspoon chopped dill

1 sage leaf, chopped, or 1 pinch dried sage

1 teaspoon freshly squeezed lemon juice

1 tablespoon pinto beans, cooked

1 tablespoon black beans, cooked

1 tablespoon white beans, cooked

1 tablespoon cooked, diced, and seeded tomato

Salt and pepper to taste

★ In a small saucepan, stir the gelatin into unheated vegetable broth and allow to sit and swell for 5 minutes. Over low heat, stir the gelatin mixture until dissolved. Remove the aspic from the heat and let rest for 4 to 5 minutes.

★ Line the terrine pan with plastic wrap. Dip each piece of roasted pepper into the aspic and place in the terrine pan in a single layer.

★ Reheat the aspic to 120°F (50°C). In another small saucepan over low heat, heat the cream cheese until melted. Add to the aspic and stir to blend. Add the remaining ingredients, stir, and adjust seasoning as needed.

★ Pour the aspic into terrine pan and chill until set, about 1 hour or overnight. Chilling overnight will allow the flavors to develop.

★ When ready to serve, unmold and slice into ¼-inch slices.
Serves 6

2 cups fish stock

4 ounces shiitake mushrooms, sliced

3 ounces shallots, minced

2 cloves garlic, minced

2 cups white wine

2 tablespoons lemon juice

1½ pounds sea bass fillets

1 cup heavy cream

4 teaspoons Dijon mustard

4 teaspoons butter

½ pound tomatoes, seeded and cut in ¼-inch dice

¼ teaspoon salt

¼ teaspoon black pepper

4 teaspoons chervil

Poached Sea Bass
WITH SHIITAKE SAUCE

★ Preheat the oven to 325°F (163°C).

★ In an ovenproof sauté pan over medium-high heat, combine the fish stock, mushrooms, all but 1 tablespoon of minced shallots, garlic, wine, and lemon juice and bring to a simmer. Place the fish in this mixture so that the sauce covers the fish halfway. Place a sheet of buttered parchment paper over the fish and place in the oven for about 7 minutes, or until the fish reaches an internal temperature of 120°F (50°C).

★ Remove the fish from the liquid and set aside in a baking pan. Return the sauté pan to the stove and reduce the liquid by three-quarters. Add the cream and reduce again until thickened to the desired consistency. Whisk in the Dijon mustard and butter.

★ In a small sauté pan, sauté the tomatoes with 1 tablespoon shallots and season with salt and pepper. Add the chervil and stir to combine.

★ Return the fish to the oven until it flakes when pressed lightly with tongs or your finger. Place the fillets on individual serving plates, dress with the sauce, and garnish with the tomato mixture. Serve immediately. *Serves 4*

8 chicken breast halves, boneless with skin on

4 tablespoons butter

7 ounces shallots, chopped

2 pounds spinach, washed and stems removed

Salt and white pepper

½ cup California zinfandel

1 cup heavy cream

4 cups chicken stock

1 teaspoon paprika

2 teaspoons salt

½ teaspoon black pepper

¼ teaspoon cayenne pepper

½ teaspoon chili powder

½ teaspoon poultry seasoning

12 tablespoons clarified butter

½ cup flour

Braised Spinach and Shallot Breast of Chicken

★ Make an incision along the side of the thickest part of the breasts and set aside.

★ In a large skillet over medium heat, melt 4 tablespoons butter, add shallots, and sauté until almost tender. Add the spinach, cover and cook until wilted. Uncover and continue cooking, stirring frequently, until the spinach is tender and liquid has boiled off. Season with salt and white pepper. Remove from skillet with a slotted spoon and set aside. Deglaze the pan with zinfandel and reduce by a quarter. Add cream, 1 tablespoon chicken stock, and reduce by about a half.

★ Remove the pan from heat and add the spinach mixture, mixing well. In another saucepan, heat the remaining chicken stock to a simmer.

★ Preheat oven to 350°F (177°C). Divide the spinach mixture into 8 equal portions and insert inside breasts. Combine the paprika, 2 teaspoons salt, black pepper, cayenne pepper, chili powder, and poultry seasoning and season both sides of the chicken breasts with this mixture. In a large skillet over medium-high heat, warm 4 tablespoons clarified butter. Add chicken breasts skin side down and sear until golden brown. Place chicken, skin side up, in a shallow roasting pan and pour in heated chicken stock to fill the pan halfway. Bake for 25 to 30 minutes or until internal temperatures reach desired doneness.

★ Remove chicken to a warm plate and cover loosely with foil. Strain the stock from the roasting pan into a measuring cup. (You should have about 1½ to 2 cups.) Keep warm.

★ Heat 8 tablespoons clarified butter in a medium saucepan over medium heat. Add flour and cook, stirring constantly until a golden brown roux forms. Gradually pour warm stock into the roux, stirring constantly, to make a smooth velouté sauce.

★ Slice each chicken breast and arrange on a plate. Spoon sauce over the top and serve. *Serves 8*

Mock Fillet of Beef

4 teaspoons whole milk

2½ slices (1½ cups) white bread, torn into pieces

2 pounds 6 ounces ground beef (25% fat)

⅛ teaspoon salt

½ teaspoon black pepper

2 tablespoons very finely chopped onion

4 teaspoons tomato juice

2 teaspoons Worcestershire sauce

⅛ teaspoon granulated garlic

16 strips raw bacon

★ Pour milk gently over torn bread pieces and set aside.

★ Combine remaining ingredients (except bacon) in a mixing bowl until thoroughly blended. Add the bread mixture and knead just until all ingredients are thoroughly incorporated. Shape into 8 round patties about 1 inch thick and wrap each patty in 2 strips of bacon, overlapping the slices and attaching the slices to the patty with toothpicks.

★ Prepare a charcoal or gas grill. Sear the patties on the grill (at about 425°F, or 218°C) for about 1 minute on each side, turning each side a quarter turn once midway through the grilling process. Arrange patties evenly spaced at least 2 inches apart on a baking sheet.

★ Preheat oven to 325°F (163°C). Bake the patties until the internal temperature reaches 150°F (66°C), about 17 minutes. Rotate the pan midway through the cooking process and drain off excess fat.

★ Remove the pan from the oven and allow to stand about 10 minutes. Remove the toothpicks and arrange the mock fillets neatly on each plate. *Serves 8*

Chocolate Pecan Pie

3 eggs, beaten

½ cup light corn syrup

½ cup sugar

½ cup semisweet chocolate chips or chopped chocolate pieces

1 tablespoon margarine, melted

1 teaspoon vanilla extract

1½ cups chopped pecans

1 (9-inch) piecrust, unbaked

★ Preheat oven to 350°F (177°C).

★ In a large bowl, mix eggs, corn syrup, sugar, chocolate, margarine, and vanilla until well blended. Blend in pecans.

★ Place the pie crust in a 9-inch pie pan. Pour the mixture into the unbaked pie shell. Trim and flute the edges of the crust. Bake for 50 to 60 minutes or until a knife inserted halfway between the center and the edge comes out clean. Cool on a wire rack before cutting into wedges and serving. *Serves 12*

White Chocolate Bread Pudding

½ cup sugar

¼ teaspoon salt

½ teaspoon cinnamon

¼ teaspoon ground nutmeg

3 cups milk, scalded and cooled slightly

3 eggs, slightly beaten

1 teaspoon vanilla extract

5 ounces (3 cups) bread cubes (firm white bread, trimmed of crust, cut into ½-inch cubes)

7 ounces white chocolate, chopped

★ Preheat oven to 350°F (177°C). Butter and flour a 2-quart mold, casserole, or soufflé dish. Set aside.

★ Combine sugar, salt, cinnamon, and nutmeg and mix well. Add sugar and spice mixture to the milk, then stir in eggs and vanilla. Add bread and chocolate and stir to combine. Pour into the prepared mold and bake for 45 to 50 minutes, or until a knife inserted near the center comes out clean. The pudding will be somewhat risen and golden brown on top. *Serves 8*

Canadian Team

Wild Mushroom Turnovers

DOUGH

8 ounces soft cream cheese

½ cup butter

2 ¼ cups flour

FILLING

8 ¾ ounces fresh wild mushrooms, cleaned and minced

1 small onion, minced

¼ cup butter

Fresh thyme leaves from 4 sprigs

2 tablespoons plus 1 teaspoon flour

½ cup sour cream, or to taste

Salt and pepper to taste

1 egg, beaten

★ Cream the dough ingredients together into a soft dough. Wrap in waxed paper and chill for 1 hour.

★ Preheat oven to 400°F (204°C). In a skillet over medium-high heat, sauté mushrooms and onion in butter until the onion is transparent. Cool slightly. In a clean bowl, blend the mushroom mixture with the thyme, flour, and sour cream and season with salt and pepper.

★ To assemble the turnovers, roll out the dough about ⅛ inch thick and cut into 2-inch squares or rounds. Place a tablespoonful of mushroom mixture in the center and brush edges with the beaten egg. Fold in half and press edges to seal. (Do not panic if they do not seal; the dough will hold.)

★ Prick the tops of the turnovers with a fork and place on a baking sheet. Bake for 12 to 15 minutes until golden brown. Serve immediately. *Makes 10 turnovers*

14 ounces crabmeat

1 teaspoon lemon juice

½ teaspoon lemon zest

3 ½ ounces bread crumbs

¼ cup mayonnaise

2 tablespoons cream cheese

1 tablespoon minced fresh chives

1 tablespoon dried parsley

1 tablespoon Cognac

Salt and pepper to taste

½ cup flour

2 egg whites

1 cup panko crumbs

1 tablespoon canola oil

VEGETABLE SLAW

1 large carrot

1 zucchini

1 teaspoon olive oil

1 tablespoon canola oil

1 teaspoon cider vinegar

1 teaspoon minced fresh basil

1 teaspoon minced fresh shallots

1 tablespoon maple syrup

1 teaspoon lemon juice

Salt and pepper to taste

SPICED AVOCADO

2 tablespoons peeled, seeded, and diced cucumber

2 tablespoons peeled and diced tomato

1 avocado, peeled

½ teaspoon minced fresh garlic

1 teaspoon fresh lime juice

1 teaspoon minced cilantro

Salt and pepper to taste

4 (3-ounce) marinated salmon slices (gravlax)

Watercress, for garnish

Marinated Salmon and Panko Crisp Crab Cake
WITH VEGETABLE SLAW AND SPICED AVOCADO

★ To make the crab cakes, carefully pick over the crabmeat in a bowl and discard any shell fragments. Combine crabmeat with the lemon juice, zest, bread crumbs, mayonnaise, cream cheese, chives, parsley, Cognac, salt, and pepper. Mix well. Divide into 4 portions and form into individual cakes. Place the flour, egg whites, and panko crumbs in separate shallow bowls. Dip each crab cake in flour, then egg whites, and then coat with the panko crumbs. Shape the cakes again, and let rest for 20 minutes.

★ In a skillet over high heat, add the oil and cook the cakes until golden on both sides. Keep hot.

★ To make the vegetable slaw, cut the carrot and zucchini into long thin strands. Blend the oils and vinegar in a food processor. Add the basil, shallots, syrup, and lemon juice. Blend this maple vinaigrette again, then season with salt and pepper.

★ To make the spiced avocado, place the diced cucumber and tomato in a stainless steel bowl. Purée the avocado flesh and garlic in a food processor. Lift out and fold into the cucumber and tomato mixture. Add the lime juice and cilantro and mix well. Season with salt and pepper.

★ To serve, arrange the salmon slices in the center of each plate. Top with a spoonful of the avocado purée, and top that with a crab cake. Toss the vegetable slaw in the maple vinaigrette and arrange on top of each crab cake. Garnish with watercress. *Serves 4*

Beef Steak Martini

½ cup gin

1 tablespoon plus 1 teaspoon vegetable oil

1 tablespoon dry vermouth

2 fresh garlic cloves, finely minced

2 fresh thyme sprigs

¼ teaspoon salt

Freshly cracked black peppercorns to taste

Dash of angostura bitters

4 (5-ounce) flank or rib eye steaks

16 stuffed green olives

★ Mix together all ingredients except the steaks and green olives. Let this marinade sit for 3 hours.

★ At the end of the 3 hours, massage marinade into meat and refrigerate for 3 hours more, flipping the steaks frequently.

★ Prepare a charcoal or gas grill. Remove the steaks from the marinade and reserve the liquid. Grill steaks to preferred doneness, brushing the meat with the reserved marinade while grilling.

★ To serve, place each steak on a plate. Garnish with olives or skewer them onto toothpicks and stick into the steaks. *Serves 4*

TIP FROM GLEN: I like to use rib eye steaks myself, and I omit the bitters. This dish goes fabulously well with fresh tomato wedges and celery slices that have been tossed in herbed vinaigrette. And of course, this tastes much better when eaten outdoors.

MARINADE FOR MUSHROOMS

2 teaspoons finely minced fresh garlic

2 teaspoons finely diced fresh shallots

¼ cup light soy sauce

¼ cup olive oil

Juice of 1 lemon

5 fresh portobello or large button mushrooms (or your favorite type)

Olive oil

3 bell peppers, 1 each of red, yellow, and green

Salt and pepper to taste

Fresh flat-leaf parsley, minced (optional)

5 (5-ounce) pork tenderloin medallions, center cut (preferably Alberta pork)

1 cup marinated green Greek olives, pitted and quartered

1 tablespoon fresh thyme leaves

6 tablespoons extra virgin olive oil

Coarse salt

10 new baby russet potatoes, boiled in salted water with thyme stalks

15 baby carrots, blanched and sautéed with honey and butter

¼ cup demi-glace

Alberta Pork Tenderloin
WITH OLIVES AND THYME

★ Prepare the marinade by whisking ingredients in a stainless steel bowl. Cut mushrooms in half and score the inner flesh with the tip of a sharp knife. Soak the mushrooms briefly in the marinade, then grill on a prepared hot barbecue grill for about 2 to 3 minutes. Put the grilled mushrooms back in the marinade and cover with plastic wrap to keep warm.

★ Preheat the oven to 350°F (177°C). Lightly oil the skin of the peppers and place them on a baking sheet. Bake for 35 to 40 minutes or until the skins are completely charred. Remove the peppers from the oven and place in a bowl. Cover the bowl with plastic wrap and set aside for about 10 minutes. Turn oven to 375°F (190°C).

★ Carefully scrape the blackened skins and inner seeds of the peppers and discard the cores. Cut the flesh into julienne strips and keep warm. Season with salt, pepper, and parsley.

★ Season the pork tenderloin medallions with salt and pepper. In a skillet over high heat, sear the pork medallions quickly on both sides. Place on a broiler pan or wire rack over a drip pan and bake until desired doneness is reached (110°F, or 44°C, internal temperature for medium rare).

★ In a nonstick sauté pan, slightly warm olive pieces just to release natural oils and flavors. Add the fresh thyme. Top each medallion with olives and thyme. Finish with a drizzle of extra virgin olive oil and a sprinkle of coarse salt.

★ To serve, in the center of each plate place a spoonful of roasted bell pepper julienne. Gently place a pork tenderloin medallion on top of the bell peppers. Set the grilled and marinated mushrooms around the medallion alternating with the carrots and baby potatoes. Finish each plate with a light drizzle of extra virgin olive oil and demi-glace, creating a slight mosaic effect with the two sauces.
Serves 5

ICE SOUFFLÉ

2 egg yolks

4 tablespoons sugar

1¼ cups heavy cream, whipped

1¼ ounces white chocolate, melted

6 tablespoons strawberry purée

LIQUID CENTER

6 tablespoons water

5 tablespoons sugar

2 teaspoons corn syrup

5 teaspoons frozen orange juice concentrate

5 teaspoons Grand Marnier

GARNISH

2½ cups fresh strawberries

¼ cup granulated sugar

⅔ cup chardonnay, such as Inniskillin chardonnay

1¼ cups seasonal berries, such as blackberries, blueberries, raspberries, or gooseberries

⅔ cup heavy cream, whipped

2 ounces shaved white or dark chocolate

12 mint sprigs

Strawberry White Chocolate Ice Soufflé
WITH A CITRUS LIQUID CENTER

★ To make the ice soufflé, warm the egg yolks and sugar in the top of a double boiler until the sugar is dissolved in the egg. Using an electric mixer or food processor, beat until cold. Fold in ⅓ of the whipped cream and melted chocolate. Fold in the remaining cream and the strawberry purée.

★ Place 12 cones (3-ounce paper cone-shaped drink cups can be used) inside plastic cups or glasses to keep them upright. Fill the cones ¾ full. Insert a second cone to form an interior cavity and freeze. Keep remaining soufflé mixture in the refrigerator to be used later.

★ To make the liquid center, combine the water, sugar, and corn syrup in a saucepan and bring to a boil. Cool the liquid and add the orange juice concentrate and Grand Marnier.

★ When the cones are frozen, twist and remove interior paper cones. Fill the center cavities with liquid center mixture, return to freezer, and let set. Seal the cone bottoms with remaining soufflé mixture and freeze overnight.

★ To prepare the garnish, clean and slice the strawberries, toss them with sugar, and add the chardonnay and your choice of berries. Let the berries and wine marinate in the refrigerator for at least 1 hour before serving.

★ To serve, remove the exterior paper cones from the frozen soufflé by dipping in warm water and squeezing. Keep the soufflé on a plate in the refrigerator for 20 minutes before serving. (This allows the liquid center a chance to defrost without melting the strawberry soufflé on the outside.)

★ Spoon a generous portion of the marinated berries and juices onto soup plates and place the strawberry soufflé on top of the berries. Spoon a dollop of whipped cream over the soufflé. (Cream can be flavored with orange or cream soda.) Sprinkle with shaved chocolate, top with a mint sprig, and serve. *Serves 12*

Singapore Team

BASIL OIL

½ cup washed and chopped fresh basil leaves

½ cup canola oil

WONTONS

4 ounces scallops

1 teaspoon chopped fresh tarragon

1 teaspoon chopped fresh chervil

Salt and pepper

4 wonton wrappers

Olive oil

6 russet potatoes, washed and peeled

4 (4-ounce) black cod fillets, skins removed

Salt and pepper

1 (10- to 12-ounce) bunch fresh spinach, washed, stems removed, and blanched

¾ cup olive oil

12 pieces sundried tomato, soaked in warm water for 10 minutes and drained

¼ cup salsify, or parsnip or carrot, peeled, sliced and blanched

¼ cup edamane (soybeans), blanched and skin removed (available in Asian specialty markets)

½ cup sweet corn kernels, steamed

½ cup snow peas, trimmed and blanched

⅓ cup aged balsamic vinegar

Fillet of Black Cod IN POTATO
CRUST AND SCALLOP WONTON

★ To make the basil oil, blend fresh basil leaves with canola oil in a food processor or blender. Pass through a fine-mesh sieve. (This may be made 2 days in advance.)

★ To assemble wontons, coarsely chop the scallops in a food processor and mix with chopped herbs. Season with salt and pepper. Place ¼ of the filling just below the center of wrapper. Fold one side over the filling and tuck its edge under the filling. Then, with a finger dipped in water, moisten exposed sides of the wrapper and roll up the filled cylinder, leaving 2 inches of the wrapper unrolled at the top. Pull the two ends of the cylinder down beneath the roll until the ends meet and overlap slightly. Pinch the ends firmly together. Cover with a dry towel. Bring water (enough to cover wontons) to a boil and drop in wontons. Return to boil, reduce heat to medium, and cook, uncovered, for 5 minutes, or until tender. Drain the wontons. Drizzle with some olive oil to prevent sticking to one another. Set aside.

★ Adjust the oven rack to middle position and preheat oven to 350°F (177°C).

★ Into a large bowl, coarsely grate the potatoes using the largest grate of a box grater. Rinse the potatoes until the water is clear.

★ Season the cod with salt and pepper and wrap with blanched spinach leaves. Drain the potatoes thoroughly and season with salt and pepper. For each fillet, place a small amount of potato on a cookie sheet, place a spinach-wrapped fillet on top and cover with another small amount of potato. In a nonstick frying pan over medium heat, pan-fry the cod in the olive oil until golden brown on both sides. Transfer the fish to a baking dish and bake for 5 to 8 minutes until fish begins to flake with a fork. Drain the fillets on paper towels and keep warm.

★ Heat the vegetables. Cut the cod fillets in half diagonally and place the 2 halves in the center of each plate. Garnish with the warm vegetables and drizzle with basil oil and aged balsamic vinegar. *Serves 4*

SHELLFISH SAUCE

10 lobster heads, cleaned

1⅜ cups unsalted butter

¼ cup corn oil

¼ cup sliced carrots

½ cup sliced onions

2 cloves garlic, peeled and crushed

7 tablespoons tomato paste

⅔ cup brandy

2 cups fish stock

1 pint cream

1 tablespoon chopped fresh tarragon

Salt and pepper

4 (¾-pound) Maine lobsters

12 clams

¾ cup trimmed and chopped asparagus (in ½-inch pieces), blanched

8 pearl onions, blanched and peeled

¼ pound purple potatoes, cubed and cooked (may substitute Red Bliss or Yukon Gold)

¼ cup peeled and chopped yellow squash (cut into matchstick strips), blanched

1 tablespoon nameko or chanterelle mushroom, sautéed

⅓ pound baby beets, trimmed, cooked and peeled

3 tablespoons olive oil

Fresh flat-leaf parsley sprigs, for garnish

Steamed Lobster and Clams WITH SHELLFISH SAUCE AND VEGETABLES

★ To prepare the sauce, in a large skillet over medium heat, sauté the lobster heads in 1 cup butter and the corn oil. Add the carrots, onion, and garlic and continue to sauté until the shells turn red and then lightly brown. Add the tomato paste and continue cooking for another 5 minutes. Flambé with brandy and add fish stock, cream, and tarragon. Simmer for 30 minutes or until sauce coats back of spoon. Strain through a fine-mesh sieve. Season the sauce to taste with salt and pepper. (This may be made a day in advance and refrigerated.)

★ Steam the whole lobsters for about 8 minutes until just cooked. Remove the claw meat and set aside. Cut off lobster tail and split in half lengthwise (do not remove meat from tail). Set aside.

★ Steam the clams separately for 5 to 6 minutes or until the clams start opening up. Discard any that don't open.

★ Reheat the sauce in a small saucepan.

★ Sauté the lobster claw meat and tail in remaining ⅜ cup butter until warm and transfer to a warm platter.

★ Sauté all the vegetables in olive oil and season to taste with salt and pepper.

★ Arrange the half lobster tails and claw meat with clams neatly on a plate and surround with the vegetables. Spoon some sauce on the lobster and garnish with fresh parsley sprigs. *Serves 4*

Pot-au-Feu of Squab
WITH AUTUMN VEGETABLES AND BLACK TRUFFLES

POACHING LIQUID

2 tablespoons chopped onion

3 tablespoons chopped carrots

3 tablespoons chopped celery

3 tablespoons chopped leeks

2 tablespoons olive oil

¼ cup dried or canned straw mushrooms*, washed and drained

2 sprigs fresh thyme

1 bay leaf

15 black peppercorns

4 cups chicken consommé

⅜ cup sherry

Salt to taste

4 (1-pound) squabs or Cornish hens, wings removed

¾ cup sliced carrots

1¼ cups Brussels sprouts, trimmed, left whole

¾ cup sliced scallions, white part only (sliced lengthwise)

¼ cup sliced shallots

2 medium (about ½ pound) Red Bliss potatoes, sliced ¼-inch thick

¼ cup hon shimeji mushrooms* or shiitake mushrooms, trimmed

¼ cup fresh or canned straw mushrooms*, halved

¼ ounce black truffles (fresh or canned), sliced, for garnish

*Found in Asian specialty markets.

★ For the poaching liquid, cook the chopped vegetables over medium heat with olive oil until golden brown. Add dried straw mushrooms, thyme, bay leaf, and peppercorns, and cook for another 5 minutes. Pour in the chicken consommé and sherry. Simmer for 40 minutes, then sieve through cheesecloth or a fine-mesh strainer. Season with salt. (This may be prepared a day in advance and refrigerated.)

★ Separate the squab legs from the carcasses. Poach the legs in poaching liquid gently for 10 minutes or until they are just cooked. Remove the legs and allow them to rest for a few minutes. Remove skin and meat from the bone, discard skin, cut meat into 1-inch cubes, and set meat aside.

★ Poach the squab breast for 6 to 7 minutes in poaching liquid. Remove the breasts and allow them to rest for 10 minutes before removing the skin and meat from the bone. Discard skin, cut meat into 1-inch cubes, and set meat aside.

★ After poaching and removing the squab, bring the liquid back to a boil, reduce heat, and cook the vegetables in this liquid, starting with the hardest vegetables to the softer ones, until tender. Add the mushrooms last.

★ Place some of the breast and leg meat in each of 4 soup plates. Divide the hot liquid with the vegetables among the plates and garnish with sliced truffles. *Serves 4*

NOTE: If using Cornish hens, cook a few minutes longer.

PINOT NOIR SAUCE

¼ cup shallots, peeled and sliced

2 tablespoons chopped carrots

2 tablespoons chopped celery

2 tablespoons olive oil

3 sprigs fresh thyme

2 cups Pinot Noir

¾ cup port wine

⅜ cup beef stock

¼ cup unsalted butter

2 (1¾-pound) French-cut racks
of lamb, fat trimmed

Salt and freshly cracked black pepper

¼ cup dried trumpet mushrooms
that have been soaked in water,
drained, and finely chopped

⅓ cup olive oil

¼ cup diced zucchini

¼ cup diced green bell pepper

¼ cup diced red bell pepper

¼ cup diced yellow bell pepper

1 tablespoon morel or porcini
mushroom, macerated in
1 tablespoon port wine

4 ounces fresh green beans,
washed, trimmed and blanched

1½ pounds sweet potatoes, roasted,
peeled, mashed, and seasoned with
salt and pepper to taste

2 tablespoons crumbled goat cheese

4 heads garlic, slow-roasted

¼ cup thinly sliced eggplant,
deep-fried, for garnish

Roast Rack of Lamb
WITH BLACK TRUMPET MUSHROOMS IN PINOT NOIR SAUCE

★ To make the Pinot Noir sauce, in a medium saucepan over high heat, cook the shallots, carrots, and celery in the 2 tablespoons olive oil for 5 minutes, or until golden brown and caramelized. Add the thyme, Pinot Noir, port, and beef stock and simmer over low heat for 35 to 40 minutes, or until reduced by a third. (This may be made 2 days in advance and refrigerated.)

★ Season the lamb racks with salt and pepper and rub the trumpet mushrooms over the lamb until well coated. Refrigerate for 1 hour before cooking.

★ Preheat the oven to 350°F (177°C). Roast the lamb rack for 15 to 20 minutes, or if you are using an instant-read thermometer, until the internal temperature reaches 130°F (54°C). Remove and allow the lamb to rest for at least 5 minutes. Debone 1 rack and cut into 8 slices for 4 portions. Cut the remaining rack into individual chops (with the bone).

★ In ⅓ cup olive oil over high heat, sauté the zucchini, peppers, morel mushrooms, and green beans for 2 minutes. Lower the heat to medium and cook 4 minutes more until cooked. Season to taste with salt and pepper.

★ Spoon warmed mashed sweet potato in the center of each plate and top with 2 slices of the deboned lamb rack and 1 cutlet. Arrange the vegetables, goat cheese, and roasted garlic around the plate and garnish with eggplant chips. Bring Pinot Noir sauce back to a boil. Remove from heat, add the unsalted butter, and stir until blended. Spoon onto lamb and serve. *Serves 4*

Acknowledgments

We'd first like to salute the extraordinary members of the U.S. Team 2000, the Canadian Team, and the U.S. Army Culinary Arts Team who contributed recipes to this book. We deeply appreciate their willingness to share their creative talents with home cooks.

We'd also like to thank the American Chefs Federation (ACF) who provided us with so much support and goodwill in our efforts to televise and document the "culinary olympics" for the first time ever. Competition kitchens and camera crews are not exactly a compatible match, but the ACF welcomed us with open arms and provided support throughout. We are especially grateful to Noel Cullen, former president of the ACF, whose faith, belief, and encouragement were with us from beginning to end.

We'd also like to thank Canada's team manager, Simon Smokowicz, who gave us access to his exceptional team and helped us understand the world of cooking competitions by patiently answering our questions and giving us an insight that only his many years of experience could offer.

We are also grateful to the wonderful people connected with the U.S. Army Culinary Arts Team who opened our eyes to the tremendous culinary talent and passion that brought this team so much gold.

Still, nothing would have been possible had it not been for the critical and generous support of two companies, Cuisinart and the Weber-Stephens Products Company, who stepped up with financial support to make the program a reality. It's not surprising, considering that both companies, like the chefs who compete, are deeply committed to quality and driven to always perform at their very best. We'd like to personally thank Paul Ackels and Mary Rodgers at Cuisinart and Michael Kempster, Sr. at Weber for their involvement and support.

We would also like to extend a big thank-you to Eschenbach Porcelain, who provided us with plates from their exquisite collection of china and to Beaulieu Vineyard for allowing us to use their beautiful kitchen to film the U.S. team.

Finally, we'd like to acknowledge PBS stations around the country and their viewers who have supported fine culinary programming for so many years now.

The Producers: Marjorie Poore and Alec Fatalevich

Index

Cooking for Gold © 2001 by Marjorie Poore Productions
Photography by Alec Fatalevich
Design: Kari Perin, Perin+Perin
Editing: Barbara King
Production: Kristen Wurz

ISBN 0-9705973-0-4
Printed in Singapore by Spectrum Pte Ltd

10   9   8   7   6   5   4   3   2   1

MPP Books, 363 14th Avenue, San Francisco, CA 94118